AQA GCSE ENGLISH LANGUAGE – PAPER 1: SECTION B: CREATIVE WRITING: 12 A STAR EXAM ANSWERS

Full mark A Star (Grade 9) Answers

By Joseph Anthony Campbell

CONTENTS

THE QUALITY CONTROL SYSTEM™ OR HOW TO GET AN A STAR!

The Quality Control System™ is fourfold.

It involves:

1) An efficient summary of the examination paper.

2) A concise focus upon the Assessment Objectives in the exam and how to approach them.

3) Clear instructions on your timings and how long you should spend on each question. ***This is the most important point of fact in this fourfold system.***

4) Further to point 3, the approximate word count per minute you should be consistently aiming for in each minute of your exam.

My students have applied all of the techniques of the Quality Control System™ I am providing you with to gain A stars (Grade 9's) in their examinations. You can replicate them by following the advice in this book. Following these rules has ensured success for my students in English Language and their other subjects and it will do for you too! The Quality Control System is explained more fully at the end of this book.

AQA ENGLISH LANGUAGE GCSE – THE BEST APPROACH TO A GRADE 9 IN CREATIVE WRITING!

The best approach for a **Grade 9** is to spend 45 to 50 minutes on each question; 40 minutes writing and 10 minutes making notes, planning and checking your final answer for basic corrections at the end of the examination.

Please be sure to describe **<u>only</u>** when asked for in your question or to alternatively write a story and to use the picture provided for your story in the examination; if you choose to write a story with the picture as a guide.

The following 12 questions and answers will help you to prepare your own Grade 9 essays and to massively improve your practice for your exams. Although your questions will of course, be different in your examination, the examples I have provided clearly demonstrate the techniques and linguistic devices expected by the AQA exam board in order to achieve a Grade 9.

This series of model answer books have helped thousands of readers to achieve their full potential!

PAPER 1: SECTION B: WRITING: FIRST ESSAY: CREATIVE WRITING COMPETITION: STORY

You are advised to spend about 45 to 50 minutes on this section.

Write in full sentences.

You are reminded of the need to plan your answer.

You should leave enough time to check your work at the end.

Question: You are going to enter a creative writing competition.

Your entry will be judged by a panel of people of your own age.

Write the opening part of a story about a place that is severely affected by the weather.

[40 Marks]

(AO5 = 24 marks for Content and Organisation; AO6 = 16 marks for Technical Accuracy)

(45/50 Minutes Total = 40 Minutes Writing + 5/10 Minutes Making Notes/Planning/Checking Final Answer for Basic Corrections)

(600 Words Maximum per Essay = 15 Words per Minute)

This vast expanse. This sand, this stillness; pervades. In isolated places, sand swirls, moving here and there, an effect of the wind upon the land. This place. This interminable heat. Water attracts life. Here, in this place, the wells ran dry, long ago. Their ornateness makes them merely ornamental and doubly impractical and useless. The sun occasionally smiles on this desert, however, now, it appears to grimace. Having no water, equals death. This endless battle, between this environment and its' inhabitants. This endless endeavour of all living beings to achieve sustenance? This desert acts as a magnet for intense heat. Does the desert desire complete singularity, to simply have only more of itself? This desert is a magnet; attracting and repelling. Without water, it attracts death and repels life.

The palm trees and their fronds, lightly sway. Once, they were former accoutrements of an oasis, and now they wait in perfect stillness and with complete patience, unperturbed as to whether water will ever once again fall from the skies and sustain them once more. At one with their fate. The sand dunes are also indifferent. Their colours change ceaselessly with the winds. The endless movement of particles of sand. This sand, moved by the capricious whims of the weather, at times perfectly peaceful and also, at times, a storm. Permanently shifting, settling and then shifting again, until the end of time. The weather created this place, melded it and moulded it, and, when it chooses, will simply destroy or re-create it.

A human body is 70% water. She was drying out like this desert. By degrees, becoming a part of its' changeless state. Even the camels were leaving. Their exodus was a harbinger of doom. Her ribs creaked. The beginning of lifeless life. The grim, resulting oppression, of months without rain. Without the intervention of life-giving water, she would become part of the singularity. Sardonically, and almost with a sense of grim satisfaction, she considered these truths.

However, she had chosen this place, or, to be more accurate, it had chosen her. One translation of 'salvation' is 'to come home' and that is how she had felt, when she had arrived and then settled, here. Jessica, who had arrived three years ago, still felt this way. To make a choice from one's own soul is to agree to whatever the decision leads to; to whatever fate befalls a person who has made such a choice. When Jessica had asked the locals, "When will it rain again?" they had looked at her with both compassion and indifference, then, shrugging their shoulders and looking up to the skies, they had calmly stated, "Inshallah". And, so, she had intuitively known that this question was beyond their scope to answer and that its answer, in turn, was beyond her comprehension.

Even now, Jessica loved this place, it's magnitude and majesty filled her with awe. As a mere mortal, she simply belonged to the land; it would and could never, belong to her or anyone else. The weather decides the fate of this place and so it would be, until the end of time.

In the distance, Jessica thought (or was it simply a fanciful imagining) that she heard the patter of tiny, infinitesimal drops of rain. Drops of life, that would lead to the saturation of this universe of sand, of this vast desert. Jessica looked up, hoping beyond hope, that this was not a cruel mockery, wondering if it was merely a mirage, as she entered the final hours of her life. Jessica, focused her attention more intently, on this vision of hope.

(600 words)

PAPER 1: SECTION B: WRITING: SECOND ESSAY: CREATIVE WRITING COMPETITION: STORY

You are advised to spend about 45 to 50 minutes on this section.

Write in full sentences.

You are reminded of the need to plan your answer.

You should leave enough time to check your work at the end.

Question: Your local newspaper is running a creative writing competition and they intend to publish the winning entries.

Write a story about two people from very different backgrounds.

[40 Marks]

(AO5 = 24 marks for Content and Organisation; AO6 = 16 marks for Technical Accuracy)

(45/50 Minutes Total = 40 Minutes Writing + 5/10 Minutes Making Notes/Planning/Checking Final Answer for Basic Corrections)

(600 Words Maximum per Essay = 15 Words per Minute)

Lieutenant Montgomery crawled across the mud, and observed that there were no signs of life.

"This wretched mud," he mused to himself. "This mud seeps through your soul, enters your veins and oozes from the pores."

All around him were corpses.

"Another foolish foray, going 'over the top'. Makes me embarrassed to be an officer. Albeit non-commissioned. Any rank above me wouldn't be seen dead here,". Lieutenant Montgomery smiled grimly as he spoke these words aloud; reasoning to himself that there was no requirement for him to be quiet.

Lieutenant Montgomery was born in 1895, of noble stock and a graduate of the 'Royal Military Academy' in Woolwich, South East London. He was said to be destined for great things and had the pedigree and the background to rise through the ranks with ease. Yet he had questioned a brigadier as regards the wisdom of an offensive against heavy German artillery and machine gun fire and voiced the fact that there was a clear inevitability of a massacre. Through this event, Montgomery found himself losing his captain's commissioned rank and his engagement to a woman of high standing. He had received the bitter disapproval of his bewildered, perhaps even shocked family and was placed, in charge of a squad of fourteen men. Yet this had focussed Montgomery's mind upon the welfare of his squad and he loved and cared about his men's safety and they loved and cared for him as they knew that he was for them and they, in turn, were for him.

Again, muttering to himself, the former captain speculated, with an exquisite sadness, "My entire squad is gone."

Suddenly there was a murmuring; signs of life!

"Private Jim!" he shouted across the barren darkness as he slithered towards him like a snake.

Private Jim was affectionately termed a 'common chap' but generally he was considered by the squad to be an estimable fellow. And he is breathing. Born from gypsy stock in 1897, he was born and raised in Liverpool. His childhood had mainly consisted of begging and occasional stays in institutions where he was detained at the King's pleasure. Then, upon his release from jail, in 1915, he had, for the first time in his young life; a plan. A plan to restore his good name and to become a part of society. He had signed up for the army and he was amazed that there were still opportunities to join up, after all, he was a former convict and the war was expected to be concluded within months. Now, Jim knew with a learned assuredness, that if this war was a part of society, that he would happily forgo a society - that could not peaceably share a continent - for the rest of his natural life. He knew, however, that his squad was a good one, all in all and that their commanding officer was one of the best around. This is why, when Lieutenant Montgomery crawled over to Private Jim Reynolds, they were equally happy to lay eyes upon one another.

The two very different backgrounds that these men were from faded further into the distance as they were the only two men still alive from their squadron of fourteen. In the mud, Lieutenant Montgomery laid a hand on Private Jim's shoulder and soothingly uttered;
"Rest easy old chap, we may still get out of this pickle yet".
Jim looked steadily at the lieutenant and with a quiet reverence replied,
"Thank you, sir, we may yet, we may yet" as the silence suddenly whistled and artillery fire emblazoned itself across the sky.

(600 words)

PAPER 1: SECTION B: WRITING: THIRD ESSAY: ONLINE COMPETITION: STORY

You are advised to spend about 45 to 50 minutes on this section.

Write in full sentences.

You are reminded of the need to plan your answer.

You should leave enough time to check your work at the end.

Question: An online competition for story writing is being held, and you have decided to enter.

Write a story with the title 'Discovery'.

[40 Marks]

(AO5 = 24 marks for Content and Organisation; AO6 = 16 marks for Technical Accuracy)

(45/50 Minutes Total = 40 Minutes Writing + 5/10 Minutes Making Notes/Planning/Checking Final Answer for Basic Corrections)

Discovery

Jenny had had a difficult week. A week in which she felt she had sung the solitary song of a lonely person in an uncaring, or at the very least, indifferent, world. She felt as if her hopes and dreams had floated away from her like balloons that have been released from inattentive children's hands. Colour had drained from the streets that she had walked upon, disintegrating into the dust, as cruel faces had leaned out from shop-fronts to tilt their heads and stare at her without remorse. Her work, had left her cold, the news had made her miserable and the disconnection she had felt had seeped into her veins. Life had lost its lustre, which was intensified and canopied by a sense of deep ennui.

Jenny had not wanted to take a walk in the park and yet, subconsciously, she knew that she was trying to discover something significant in the everyday reality of taking a stroll. It was the beginning of spring; winter was finally releasing its icy hold and relinquishing to nature's renewal. As she entered the park, she noticed a red breasted robin perched upon a maple tree, fluttering back and forth. As she looked intently at the beauty of the robin, for the first time she felt truly connected to a bird and felt as if it had been sent to balm her troubled soul.

As Jenny witnessed the changing formation of the clouds, she thought to herself, 'The clouds are balls of cotton.' Taking a sip of water as she walked, leaves and twigs cracked underfoot. There were patches of a deep blue sky showing through the clouds that had met and accumulated as delicate flowers rose to meet the resplendent rays of the sun. The flowers themselves appeared to have an innate awareness of their own transcendent, otherworldly beauty as Jenny gazed at the chrysanthemums. The wind whispered its song delicately through the trees as they danced in the resulting breeze.

The sunlight was glinting off the leaves and as they caught the light, the shifting light, the colours refracted; dazzling, spangling, golden leaves, and the sunlight was appearing on the lake like crystals, dotted all around, constantly moving, everywhere and nowhere at once. The grass was as soft as a snail trail as Jenny heard the notes of sparrows twittering in unison. Visible in the approaching twilight were evergreens and trees as tall as towers; an impregnable domain. Jenny hearkened intently to the birds and gazed at the large shiny leaves of the cherry-laurel bushes. At the almost exact same moment, an open secret was revealed to her, whispered lightly upon the gentle wind: 'Speech is like silver, but silence is golden'.

As she observed the setting sun, Jenny mused, 'Yet, even gold changes but within, I've got diamonds!'. She was now intuitively aware that she would be leaving behind nights of fear and doubt and that they would inevitably give way to a wondrously clear daybreak: The new day; the source and perfection of life itself.

This was sacred to Jenny's heart; the magnificence and beauty of nature! A beautiful treasure amongst the mediocre creations of man. A piece of bliss amongst the gloom and now once more, she was witness to an epiphany, experiencing a metamorphosis from a chrysalis of despair. The renaissance of hope, a long-forgotten memory, once more rekindled her hope in the future. Jenny knew with clarity that she was discovering something of significance. Jenny felt the radiance of angels shining upon her. Through this discovery, her tears became a river, flowing from grateful eyes.

(600 words)

PAPER 1: SECTION B: WRITING: FOURTH ESSAY: CREATIVE WRITING: WEBSITE: STORY

You are advised to spend about 45 to 50 minutes on this section.

Write in full sentences.

You are reminded of the need to plan your answer.

You should leave enough time to check your work at the end.

Question: Your school or college is asking students to contribute some creative writing for its website.

Write a story about a magical world.

[40 Marks]

(AO5 = 24 marks for Content and Organisation; AO6 = 16 marks for Technical Accuracy)

(45/50 Minutes Total = 40 Minutes Writing + 5/10 Minutes Making Notes/Planning/Checking Final Answer for Basic Corrections)

By Joseph Anthony Campbell

(600 Words Maximum per Essay = 15 Words per Minute)

He was a space adventurer, a mercenary, or a soldier of fortune, as he liked to be known, flying through a violent thunderstorm as crumbling thunder and lightning flashed across the sky. Entering a world of dark light, the engine of his ship whined as the stars looked on indifferently, sparkling like diamonds. He thought, 'It could not happen, surely' as a meteor appeared to rise and meet him. Swerving sharply to his starboard side, the ship spiralled through the ether, seeking safety and salvation. This soldier of fortune, remembered unfaded memories as he prepared to face his end and quietly said to himself before the moment of impact, 'once we dreamed, now we have come to the end of the seam, of magic that has finally run out.' Crashing into an underground lake, man and cargo plunged into the black waters, deep underwater, pushed and pulled by the certain movement of tides through clumps of green slime. The end of a plunging voyage. The lake led to circular rivers as the wind blew fiercely, waves traversing across and slapping the edges of the bodies of water; like a miniature sea.

Yet, there was a spark within, a strange, solitary sensation. Pulling toward him, like an invisible cord, magic was not beyond his reach. Hope embodied as figures with magical charms and powers and these mermaids of the lake, spread like a net, their senses keen and their intentions noble, talked to one another under the water. The ladies of the lake; beautiful protectors! He was transported to a breathing hole and found his way through the icy surface of the lake. His breath returned alongside his once desperate hope. The ship was now moving over to him, fully restored, unstoppable, unsinkable; transported by the mermaids along an invisible line. The pools of water dried instantly at his feet; he was swiftly led by the mermaids into a sealed-off world. As he looked out across the glittering kingdom in front of him, he took in a sharp intake of breath. The light from the sky was butter-gold. On his face, came a sudden smile. His perception was both exalted and clear.

The magical world he now observed reflected back to him a golden age of creativity. Magic reawakened within him as he experienced the precise moment of an epiphany.

He had not only an emotional response but a physical, mental and spiritual one to this magical world.

In the evening light he was presented before a woman who was declared by the mermaids as the 'Goddess of Victory'. Her vast palace was a sight to behold, labyrinthine and containing multitudinous and vastly differing delights within. There were intricately detailed tapestries, balustrades as tall as towers, leading to the finest furniture in ornate, perfumed rooms, lit by tall, golden candelabras and great drawing-rooms covered in satin and silk. Exquisite dishes were served on golden plates with gleaming silverware reflecting mythical figures. And, finally, the most transcendent sight; the 'Goddess' herself, in ropes of pearls, gold and magnificent diamonds exuding glorious purpose and presence.

Her victorious beauty provided peace within his heart.

This was liberation. He experienced the very strangeness of freedom as she presented him with a gold and silver-plated chalice. He was drinking the very elixir of life! At once, he entered a kind of trance and felt that at any moment vapour would rise from his lips; as if he might suddenly turn to air.

Then, suddenly, the entire scene scrambled back and forth incessantly as the child firmly shook her snow globe and the magical world contained within.

(600 words)

PAPER 1: SECTION B: WRITING: FIFTH ESSAY: CREATIVE WRITING COMPETITION: DESCRIPTION

You are advised to spend about 45 to 50 minutes on this section.

Write in full sentences.

You are reminded of the need to plan your answer.

You should leave enough time to check your work at the end.

Question: Your local newspaper is running a creative writing competition and the best entries will be published.

Describe life as you imagine it in 200 years' time.

[40 Marks]

(AO5 = 24 marks for Content and Organisation; AO6 = 16 marks for Technical Accuracy)

(45/50 Minutes Total = 40 Minutes Writing + 5/10 Minutes Making Notes/Planning/Checking Final Answer for Basic Corrections)

(600 Words Maximum per Essay = 15 Words per Minute)

On a vast floating neon billboard are written the words,
'2222! The year of all the 2s! A once in a millennium occurrence!'
Cars, hovercrafts, and even spacecraft are journeying to space and jostle for position in a vastly overcrowded sky as they narrowly avoid each other and the billboard, and traverse through the atmosphere. They are all driverless and rapid; humans on Earth are now passengers only, deemed unworthy and incapable of avoiding accidents. Only androids are considered proficient and capable enough to be allowed to take control of any form of vehicular conveyance. The vehicle lights appear to wink at each other as they approach one another and yet occasionally, the android controlled and driverless vehicles crash and become enflamed in mid-air. The sound is drowned out by violent thunderstorms which rage overhead as the occasional burst of acidic rain falls from the sky, like teardrops.

Artificially intelligent vacuums, manned by robotic arms, hum happy tunes as they clean the detritus and radioactive waste from the city streets; the after-effects of a fairly recent nuclear fallout. Space tourism and the more expensive time travel tourism agencies advertise their services from hologrammatic virtual reality advertisements projected from 1000-foot skyscrapers. Space tourism is a burgeoning industry as post-colonial worlds within the solar system can be travelled to for those who have the means and are thus fortunate enough to escape the water and oxygen shortages and the plethora of viruses circulating on Earth. Time-travel tourism allows those who partake in this relatively new phenomenon to observe and participate in past events through a virtual reality simulator that mirrors actual reality in every sense, except people and androids are unable to affect the time-space continuum and the events of the past.

Dark light reflects human faces as they scurry along and giggle, growl, murmur, whine and whisper. Negotiation is commonplace amongst the entirely hazmat suited human population, with people trading oxygen for a signal to the 'Universal Net', which completely captures the attention of the people plugged into it and transports them to alternative and much more pleasant realities.

In the centre of this landscape, there is a vast compound with a 100-storey palace surrounded by hard light; which encircles the palace and resembles a row of white daggers. There are long, narrow opulent terraces emitting shafts of light that are almost celestial in appearance as electrified laser structures mark off the boundaries of all of the palatial territories. A single, solitary spire of pure silver protrudes from the rooftop, like an ivory tusk. The President's palace stands defiantly and creates within the people a grim paradox, as the remaining humans' worship and revere their all-powerful president, (who is a product and creation of the unification of humanity and technology) however, they are also equally fearful of the Presidents rule and laws. There is a 500-foot hologrammatic image of the President who states through surround sound - that dominates all frequencies and interrupts all alternative signals – that, 'Technology, when correctly and appropriately understood, possesses not only all truth but all beauty. Therefore, humankind is justified in following all of its dictates.'

Outside, jailers load their prisoners into vast transportation vehicles, to become part of the 'singularity'; the vast merging of human consciousness with the technology it once created and had a degree of control over. Yet, on the fringes of Earth's atmosphere, lie the space vehicles of the 'Resistance', a combination of a sizeable number of androids and humans operating military spacecrafts who fully oppose the Presidents totalitarian rule and who believe with all of their hearts that hope still remains.

(600 words)

PAPER 1: SECTION B: WRITING: SIXTH ESSAY: CREATIVE WRITING: WEBSITE: STORY

You are advised to spend about 45 to 50 minutes on this section.

Write in full sentences.

You are reminded of the need to plan your answer.

You should leave enough time to check your work at the end.

Question: Your school or college is asking students to contribute some creative writing for its website.

Write a story with the title 'Abandoned'.

[40 Marks]

(AO5 = 24 marks for Content and Organisation; AO6 = 16 marks for Technical Accuracy)

(45/50 Minutes Total = 40 Minutes Writing + 5/10 Minutes Making Notes/Planning/Checking Final Answer for Basic Corrections)

(600 Words Maximum per Essay = 15 Words per Minute)

Abandoned!

He awoke in the chasm of the mountain. He was enveloped by darkness. The wind howled ceaselessly, mirroring his inner turmoil. The pain of being abandoned was unbearable. Yet, as he began to accept the truth of this painful fact, he felt that all of his immediate experience will be much easier to comprehend; in relation to this painful separation and abandonment.

Tentatively, he opened his eyes and took in his surroundings. With each movement of his sinews, there was the sound of creaking and cracking. With tremendous effort, he appraised himself: He was exposed and starved on this mountain. He was covered by the earth. He lifted his head and met the air. The sensation he felt immediately was of much needed oxygen flooding through his body. He gasped and drank it in. Then, slowly, his heart rate and his breathing became steadier. The chasm itself, however, seemed to be rejecting his attempt at survival.

His cloak was torn, a once treasured possession, and the pins were now loose and unfastened. In his mind, he had become the cloak, felt that he too, had become like a discarded item. He coolly observed the fact that the blood had dried on his body and reasoned that he must have spent many hours in this chasm. Physically, he was not as damaged as he had feared but his left leg would need medical attention as soon as possible. He placed his hand upon his head and felt the physical abrasions at the centre of his skull. Here, at the bottom of this decaying chasm, he could feel his consciousness drifting. Here, at the jaws of death, he had descended within himself.

Yet hope was kindled from such dire circumstances. Immediately, he accepted his reality. He knew that he must direct the little energy and mental focus he had to the task at hand; survival. He knew once more that he must accept this moment, the reality that he currently faced and that he was in and that he must not resist it; for he knew that resistance combined with weakness led to death. Suddenly, another thought burned within him, a thought that entirely sublimated the chasm that had temporarily become his home. A thought that arose within his awareness and soared above his present circumstance. For he remembered and intuitively knew once more that the mind was the ultimate decider of a man's destiny. His mind now focused on a single objective; leaving this chasm alive! Nothing else remained in his awareness. He found the courage deep within himself to persevere and concentrated his thoughts solely on overcoming this chasm. He could emerge from this place. This pain would lead to scars that would, in turn, ultimately heal. He repeated to himself, and the thought echoed within, that he could overcome this situation. This path, this abandonment, had led him to this exact moment. And this, he decided, would now be a form of chrysalis, from which he would re-emerge stronger. A strength born from this intense but momentary, weakness.

He observed a dim spark of light in the distance, he knew that beyond the dark side of the centre of this mountain range, there was light. There was a dim spark of hope. He took a deep breath and fixed his eyes upon this point of light in the distance where the light flickered.

Now, it was his body's turn to match his intentions. Eventually, he lifted himself, walked forward and slowly climbed out of hell.

He then knew with certainty that he would claw his way to survival!

(600 words)

PAPER 1: SECTION B: WRITING: SEVENTH ESSAY: CREATIVE WRITING COMPETITION: STORY

You are advised to spend about 45 to 50 minutes on this section.

Write in full sentences.

You are reminded of the need to plan your answer.

You should leave enough time to check your work at the end.

Question: Your local library is running a creative writing competition. The best entries will be published in a booklet of creative writing.

Write a story about an event that cannot be explained.

[40 Marks]

(AO5 = 24 marks for Content and Organisation; AO6 = 16 marks for Technical Accuracy)

(45/50 Minutes Total = 40 Minutes Writing + 5/10 Minutes Making Notes/Planning/Checking Final Answer for Basic Corrections)

(600 Words Maximum per Essay = 15 Words per Minute)

Jasmine's heart was beating rapidly as she approached the bridge. Soft billows of smoke were rising from the small, ancient dwellings of Kuanda village that Jasmine was now finally escaping from. To the west of her, traces of a wintry sun hung low in the sky, permanently defying the onset of spring. The beginnings of a snowstorm fell all around her and the bridge was already blanketed in snow and ice. There was clear distress in her eyes.

The dilapidated Kuandinsky Bridge had a six-foot-wide path and no railing to protect Jasmine from falling into the icy depths of the Vitim River below. It had a disintegrating metal structure and it was covered by rotting wooden planks which were incredibly slippery due to the ever-present snow and ice. Jasmine had occasionally witnessed people in their vehicles, (who were brave enough to cross the bridge) and how the passengers had had to frantically roll the windows down in order to prevent the harsh winds from throwing the vehicles, and the passengers within; off the bridge. The bridge was a rickety decaying structure which had been abandoned for three decades and it was in a complete state of disrepair. Jasmine could clearly discern a collection of gaping holes surrounding the central beam which exposed the frozen depths below. Adding further to her sense of terror were fierce winds which threatened to throw Jasmine from the 1,870-foot bridge into the watery, icy depths below. Jasmine was a realist and used to coldly calculating the odds and she reasoned that she had a miniscule chance of crossing this dilapidated, snow- and ice-covered bridge in the midst of a snowstorm and that crossing this bridge would most likely lead to her doom. Yet, the thought that, 'slavery is the antithesis of freedom,' came to the forefront of her mind and she knew definitively that crossing the bridge was the only choice for her. Jasmine steeled herself and began to cross the rotting Russian roadway.

Jasmine took her first steps away from Kuanda village and its 1500 inhabitants, precariously navigating the icy wooden planks and her hands shook as she picked her way across. The conditions were unnerving as she attempted to traverse the bridge and plumes of spray, leaping and wide, were welling and swelling with the tide upon the unfrozen parts of the river below. The other side of the bridge appeared as almost something sacred and holy to Jasmine in her current plight. The whine of the rotting planks was equally adrenaline-inducing and terrifying to Jasmine. And then suddenly she thought, 'Something isn't right here' and in almost exactly the same moment Jasmine teetered off the edge of the bridge and began to fall, spiralling downwards, futilely seeking safety. In her mind's eye, she saw herself falling through white daggers of snow and ice and into the stormy river which raged all around her and then eventually consumed her as the indifferent bridge looked on.

And then, suddenly, as she fell in unison with the snowflakes, a presence with long flowing hair like a golden river and icy blue eyes lifted her to safety, through the gaping holes of the Kuandinsky Bridge's central beam, and then hovering above it, led her to the other side of the bridge. This presence moved like an amber bird and had the radiance of an angel. And then as quickly as this divine presence had appeared, it withdrew from human sight. An inexplicable event had occurred to Jasmine. And after a quick prayer of gratitude on her knees, Jasmine rose and continued her desperate escape; journeying onwards.

(600 words)

PAPER 1: SECTION B: WRITING: EIGHTH ESSAY: CREATIVE WRITING: WEBSITE: DESCRIPTION

You are advised to spend about 45 to 50 minutes on this section.

Write in full sentences.

You are reminded of the need to plan your answer.

You should leave enough time to check your work at the end.

Question: Your school or college is asking students to contribute some creative writing for its website.

Describe a place you think is beautiful.

[40 Marks]

(AO5 = 24 marks for Content and Organisation; AO6 = 16 marks for Technical Accuracy)

(45/50 Minutes Total = 40 Minutes Writing + 5/10 Minutes Making Notes/Planning/Checking Final Answer for Basic Corrections)

(600 Words Maximum per Essay = 15 Words per Minute)

The cabin. Surrounded by a white blanket of snow. The wind sings its solitary song, snow falls like leaves. The stars wink and generously give their glow which emanates from the clear night sky. The moon, too, is fulsome and bright, interweaving between clouds, lighting the cabin naturally, travelling through the large windows within. The moon is dutifully replaced by the sun at daybreak, its' rays glinting off the snow. The fire is lit inside, its warmth provides comfort, the logs burn with a hiss and a crackle, shooting sparks before eventually becoming embers. The trees here stand as tall as gothic towers. A black bear wanders past, its' fur contrasting sharply with the ice. A beautiful sight. The wolves whine and only very occasionally, growl. In between the sounds, the silence speaks.

The cabin is an hour northeast of the city. Cold and beautiful, a world away from soaring house prices and everyday concerns. A rural and rustic timber-frame cabin. The land is pristine, snow-covered yet wild, the cabin is set amongst many acres. Here, in November, the beginning of winter, in this cabin and on this land; it is a place of beauty. Amongst the wolves, wild turkeys, bears and deer. Inside, there is kindling for the fire, freshly chopped wood - gratefully transported to the cabin - which provides a future promise of warmth and comfort.

Deer frolic nearby despite the wintry scene. Again, the wild bear wanders, perhaps drawn to the fire from within the cabin or to the stew. A hot meal to counteract the cold. All tasks have been completed, the wood is gathered, the brush is cleared and the lumber stacked. The walls have been put up in the barn. This cabin, amongst this land and in this wintry scene, provides an opportunity to escape society and all its accompanying roles and responsibilities. A place to reside and find solace in the dead of winter.

Winter. It bleeds into the soul naturally. No sound except the sound of your own thoughts, eventually and mercifully drowned out by the totality of the silence. Isolated, in winter, the singularity of being in this cabin and in these woods, where their beauty holds new fascinations to be revealed each day. Awaking each morning at dawn, as sunlight reflects from the white brilliance of the snow. Hazy days, merging and melding together with one another.

The haunting wildness, of those branches. The trees, no leaves, startling white – always breathtakingly beautiful. This is not a place of powerful, at times, intimidating mountains and oceans. Here, there is a subtler, gentler beauty; lakes, trees and fields and now they are covered and cosseted by the snow and ice. All is preserved throughout winter. In this place, one is but a solitary figure amongst the bare branches; at one with snowy isolation.

Acres of land, richly abundant with trees and wildlife. The honest labour, chopping wood to provide kindling, and fetching water, clears your head and provides new avenues of inspiration. An inquisitive, introverted time of internal thinking. The pines are so tall, resembling Jack's beanstalk. The light traverses inside and around them. The bare hills and branches reveal the ever present and vast space in between. That space filters within, giving a sense of freedom.

Then, by March, winter draws to a close. Eventually, emerging from the mystical, magical cabin; its comfort has banished loneliness; creating a fully realised catharsis. You can arrive at the cabin in a broken state and leave it whole.

Winter, in this cabin, amongst this land, is a beautiful thing in a beautiful place.

(600 words)

PAPER 1: SECTION B: WRITING: NINTH ESSAY: CREATIVE WRITING COMPETITION: STORY

You are advised to spend about 45 to 50 minutes on this section.

Write in full sentences.

You are reminded of the need to plan your answer.

You should leave enough time to check your work at the end.

Question: Your local newspaper is running a creative writing competition and the best entries will be published.

Write a story about time travel.

[40 Marks]

(AO5 = 24 marks for Content and Organisation; AO6 = 16 marks for Technical Accuracy)

(45/50 Minutes Total = 40 Minutes Writing + 5/10 Minutes Making Notes/Planning/Checking Final Answer for Basic Corrections)

(600 Words Maximum per Essay = 15 Words per Minute)

Jason had made the technological leap after nineteen months of devoted effort and had succeeded in creating a simulator that could travel through time without affecting the time-space continuum. He now just had to confirm the details with the highly secretive government agency that he was working for and immediately submit the prototype according to their strict instructions. Jason was a portrait of a man in transition; his youth was behind him and his elder years ahead.

As Jason prepared to submit his work, a memory occurred to him from the turn of the millennium and even the memory of her lovely voice was music to his ears. The thought of her sweet smile consumed him and he reasoned that he could visit the year 2000 and see her one last time. He knew with assuredness that he was unable to interfere with the space-time of the past and yet, he also knew that his prototype had not been rigorously tested by a peer group of fellow accomplished scientists.

Jason, setting the spacetime coordinates, took a deep breath and then transported himself through time. His environment shifted, coalesced, dilapidated and reformed and Jason found himself outside in central London. Instinctively, intuitively, he knew there had been a problem. As a young boy rang a bell and called out 'Man to be hung outside Newgate Prison today, for the vile crime of shoplifting' whilst selling newspapers, Jason knew from the boy's words and attire that there had been a miscalculation. As he exchanged his watch for a copy of 'The Sunday Times', his fears were confirmed as he read the printed date state, '27th of November 1822.' His mathematical calculations had been off by almost a factor of 10! Yet, he knew he was fortunate, he may have arrived in a time before the human race existed!

Jason reasoned however, that he could always return to his former present time through the time travel simulator located in his pocket. Therefore, he walked around for a few hours in the time of King George IV and passed the Wellington Monument which had been inaugurated in honour of the seventh anniversary of the duke's victory at Waterloo. He also visited the Royal Academy of Music and listened to people excitedly discussing the recent discovery of a fossil. He remembered from his past schooldays, that this was the year Percy Bysshe Shelley had died, a poet he greatly admired. More importantly, he remembered hieroglyphs had been deciphered through the 'Rosetta Stone', which through its revelation of previously undiscoverable mysteries, had created within him his initial childhood urges to decipher the mystery of time travel.

Then came another memory of her, which he took as a sign, and steeling himself, he set the simulator and was convinced through thorough inspection that he would now arrive in the year 2000 and see her once more. Once again, the London streets shifted, coalesced, dilapidated and reformed and after a period of deafening silence, he found himself in the midst of a violent thunderstorm as lightning danced across the sky and acidic rain fell, hissing from the sky. He coughed, wheezed and found it hard to breathe. In the distance, Jason could discern from a vast floating neon billboard the inscription, '2222!'. Sighing to himself, yet pleasantly resigned, he once again took the simulator from his pocket and resolved to find her, regardless of the consequences, as the instructions of the government agency that had employed him – for the creation of a time machine simulator – completely evaporated and were submerged and overtaken by the memory of her.

(600 words)

PAPER 1: SECTION B: WRITING: TENTH ESSAY: CREATIVE WRITING: MAGAZINE: DESCRIPTION

You are advised to spend about 45 to 50 minutes on this section.

Write in full sentences.

You are reminded of the need to plan your answer.

You should leave enough time to check your work at the end.

Question: A magazine has asked for contributions for their creative writing section.

Write a description of an old person.

[40 Marks]

(AO5 = 24 marks for Content and Organisation; AO6 = 16 marks for Technical Accuracy)

(45/50 Minutes Total = 40 Minutes Writing + 5/10 Minutes Making Notes/Planning/Checking Final Answer for Basic Corrections)

(600 Words Maximum per Essay = 15 Words per Minute)

Despite his age, he still had a relatively strong physical composition. For many years now, he had refrained from excess, ate modestly, lived a life of discipline and applied himself patiently and diligently to life's tasks. Yet, eventually, age had left its marks upon him, travelling from within the core of his being to the outer remnants of his physical body. His hair, once black, then a mixture of black and grey, and now white, reflected the portrait of a man beyond transition. His youth was long behind him and now he was at the end of his elder years. The crevices and pores of his face bore witness to the many winters he had endured and the cold winds that had blown in from the sea and slowly yet irrevocably weathered and then ravaged his features.

The oxygen didn't flow in as easily now, the bones creaked with overuse and pleaded for the cessation of duty. He had to admit to himself, somewhat reluctantly that yes, there was a loss here. A constriction of a once experienced freedom. The freedom of being able to breathe deeply and easily without any strain or effort. For too long, he had experienced this discomfort and now his discomfort was nearing its end.

Yet the eyes were clear, ageless, pools of memory, storing the many events of his life. His eyes, reflected the wisdom and the losses he had experienced. They held the key to his innermost nature and essence. His mind now took precedence over his body. He experienced the sensations of his inner feelings and reflections much more acutely than his physical body now. This shell, this impermanent vehicle of experience. He knew there were deeper realities than the reality of this life; this life that was now ending for him. The race had now been run and mainly, he was relieved.

His life, he often pondered, was but one of countless lives, merely one human experience coming to an end as others simultaneously ended and began. He considered himself fortunate. He had experienced remarkable events in this life.

As a younger man, a man in the prime of his physical life, he had always been gnawed and assailed by doubts. He had anxiously fretted over whether he would experience the personally significant events that make a life. Moments, mere moments perhaps, he had thought, but once experienced they were treasure chests of human experience that no thief could break in and steal. They were preserved in memory. Untouchable. Later, when he had been fortunate enough to experience these long sought after and desired moments, he had been able to finally relax and accept the onslaught of inexorable aging that assails all life and thus he remained in a state of patient readiness towards the eventual end that must inevitably come. Burning or rusting out, each person's light must eventually be extinguished.

Reflecting again, on years gone by and moments that were not faithfully preserved by memory, it was the feelings he experienced when he thought of her that were most visceral, the most reliable indicators for him. This memory transcended the ravages of old age that now affected his body. He smiled wanly but with a depth of feeling as he remembered her. The reality of their connection transcended this mortal experience. Their lonely lives, had been temporarily conjoined. Together, briefly, but in moments that would forever remain, he had experienced oneness with another human.

As his consciousness left him, the vision of that face shrouded his inner vision.
A face more divine than human; the vision of her face.

(600 words)

PAPER 1: SECTION B: WRITING: ELEVENTH ESSAY: ONLINE COMPETITION: STORY

You are advised to spend about 45 to 50 minutes on this section.

Write in full sentences.

You are reminded of the need to plan your answer.

You should leave enough time to check your work at the end.

Question: An online competition for story writing is being held, and you have decided to enter.

Write a story, set in a mountainous area.

[40 Marks]

(AO5 = 24 marks for Content and Organisation; AO6 = 16 marks for Technical Accuracy)

(45/50 Minutes Total = 40 Minutes Writing + 5/10 Minutes Making Notes/Planning/Checking Final Answer for Basic Corrections)

(600 Words Maximum per Essay = 15 Words per Minute)

A breath-taking landscape! The sheer presence of mountains, leading to magnificent peaks, rolling into valleys; endless, ever-present mountains. Millions of years ago - landmass once collided into landmass and the result of all of this gathered earth and rock, led to the creation of ridges, peaks, valleys, waterways and mountains. The rocks, to some, may seem indifferent yet mountains observed correctly, he mused, are monuments to truth and supreme beauty.

When he was but a child, in his simple room, he had watched the mountains appear to rise and cordially meet the moon. He would often wonder what lay beyond the mountains?

Here and now, 5000 metres above sea level, the winter air is bracing. Here, at the edge of the earth is a convulsion of mountains and what lays beyond is the plateau; the specific point to which he is now headed. His journey has not been without difficulty. He has travelled many days, through villages, footpaths, and fields, climbing steadily from the river and merging into the forest.

The wind is like a howling wolf and the snow, a blanket, soft like velvet, crumpling and crunching comfortably underfoot. He has been climbing and hiking through terrain of different heights and geometry and wedged himself between rocks; dangling upon precarious ledges of multitudinous mountains.

There is endless space below. Narrow passages and vistas that go beyond the limited scope of his vision. Rocks of infinite shape and size are piled upon one another. Climbing and traversing the mountain face he has witnessed the sky pushing onto the land below whilst moving amongst the cloudbanks. At one point, he had a bad fall and he had grimaced and growled before allowing his mind to command his body and lead him to safety through the boulders and rocks that are part of, and one with, the majestic mountain. Beautiful and difficult moments interspersed and interwoven together.

Precisely unscrewing the top off his water bottle, he drinks the contents within and takes in the scene before him. The sky overhead is an endless expanse; overarching and surrounding the mountainside. The flowers on the trail, remind him of the grace and benevolence of mother nature. His determination has enabled him to overcome the intense and challenging conditions he has encountered. His continued persistence has provided the momentum needed. Tired and aching, he has been constantly and consistently perplexed by an internal dilemma; whether to quit or forge ahead. Occasionally, he has lost his breath and wheezing, could hardly breathe. He has had to rely on an inner grit and determination, to travel towards and discover, at last, something significant. At times, he has felt drawn forward by an unseen force, of finding something that is at this moment, only his to discover. A hoped-for destiny, soon to be realised. Smiling, now, he realises that forging ahead was his only choice.

Reaching the plateau, in between these domineering and powerful mountains, suddenly and irrevocably, the discovery of a pristine lake creates within him a spiritual and mystical enlightenment. A metaphorical discovery. The discovery of the wordless beauty of nature, which leaves him, in turn, speechless. The calm lake is a mirror, reflecting back to him his innermost and true self. He speculates and briefly understands the magnificence of the unknowable universe and the real importance of loving and being loved. All these thoughts are reflected back to him from the lake as he merely and simply sits in silence and experiences its utter profundity. In this moment, the vanity and loneliness of his life disappears as he finally and fully realises what lies beyond.

(600 words)

PAPER 1: SECTION B: WRITING: TWELFTH ESSAY: CREATIVE WRITING COMPETITION: DESCRIPTION

You are advised to spend about 45 to 50 minutes on this section.

Write in full sentences.

You are reminded of the need to plan your answer.

You should leave enough time to check your work at the end.

Question: Your local library is running a creative writing competition. The best entries will be published in a booklet of creative writing.

Write a description of a mysterious place.

[40 Marks]

(AO5 = 24 marks for Content and Organisation; AO6 = 16 marks for Technical Accuracy)

(45/50 Minutes Total = 40 Minutes Writing + 5/10 Minutes Making Notes/Planning/Checking Final Answer for Basic Corrections)

(600 Words Maximum per Essay = 15 Words per Minute)

Here, the moon plays hide and seek with the clouds as the leaves wave in the wind. A lonely, cold place. Rain falls softly like teardrops from sullen clouds and lands on indifferent stones. The wind hisses and whines intermittently between long periods of deafening silence. The living dead reside here, ghosts of memories past, too early for entrance to heaven, and yet too hopeful for entrance to hell. Her skin is cold as ice as she glimpses the darkness; the endless inescapable darkness. The mysterious darkness of shadows and undergrowth, rolling over hills and moorland. The darkness that becomes part of your being. The darkness you will never be without. Branches that resemble mangled faces, clawed hands, diseased limbs; rustling and creeping, leaping out, emerging from the darkness. Mysteries you cannot quite discern, shifting and dissipating on the wind.

Once, in this place, there was the lighting of fires, mellow bells and angry words fired out like bullets. Hearts full of cold iron. It is said that people hear them talking still, voices travelling along the harsh winds, emanating from the trees. Dark foxes have gone to ground as the flowers grow in concrete gardens. There is a presence, pale and anxious, moving furtively among the massive mangled branches, calling on the wind; reaching out across the moors.

The gnarled growth, throws solitary, twisted shadows, across the undergrowth. Trunks of snarling, tangled trees lead to a heavily padlocked door and old glass windows blunt and distort the images created by the howling moors. Long gone memories, slowly withdrawing. Wrought-iron gates lead to dull red bricks and flat stones where brick buttresses run from east to west, forming a southern boundary. Once, there stood a churchyard with a tall, gleaming spire and there were public gardens. A long narrow set of mean, dilapidated stables remain and a narrow courtyard with a high wall which once separated it from the old churchyard. In the centre of this place lies a four-storey brick building with brick houses and brick barracks contained within; surrounded and closed off by iron gates. Inside, multitudinous windows in various states of disrepair and wooden floors lead to a fireplace. The rooms within are filled with deep cupboards on either side of the fireplace: these cupboards once provided ample storage and contained coal, cooking utensils, and the clothes of its former occupants. She noticed certain, specific dark marks on the wooden floors as she looked wistfully upon the rooms in which people had lived and died. There are no internal hallways, rooms were once accessed directly from the outside via wooden staircases which lead to a kitchen and a public and private room. The stairs groan as she walks upon them and the doors protest, even when they are opened slowly and carefully. Opening the cellar doors leads to a couple of rooms, places of former anguish where once there was an easement of irons for the occupants who resided within. In the attic of this building, there was no easement to be found.

She exits the building through the turreted front lodge, and steps lightly and gingerly upon the paving-stones of the now extinct institution; very little altered if at all. Residing within are the ghosts of former years; their misery encapsulated. Ivy weaves around fences, drooping downwards, deeply entangled, as she walks by the edges of the dark reach of the spinney.

Here, in this place of deep mystery, within its cage and in this place of ancient secrets, is a former witness to grave events; forever condemned to conceal past horrors and to forgo peace.

(600 words)

TOP TIPS FOR A GRADE 9 IN THE CREATIVE WRITING SECTION

In your answer, it is best to use as many of the following **10** linguistic techniques and devices as possible. I have used them repeatedly throughout each of the 12 Grade 9 answers I have created and provided for you in this book.

1. **Simile** – compares using 'as' or 'like'; e.g., 'white as snow'.
2. **Metaphor** – uses an image or idea to become something else; e.g., 'The classroom was a zoo.'
3. **Personification** – a metaphor attributing human feelings to an object; e.g., 'Lightning danced across the sky.'
4. **Onomatopoeia** – words sound like the noises they represent; e.g., 'The leaves cracked and crunched underfoot.'
5. **Alliteration** – repetition of letters and sounds in a series of words; e.g., 'The ship spiralled, seeking safety.'
6. **Oxymoron** – a phrase that combines two or more contradictory words; e.g., 'deafening silence'.
7. **Antithesis** – putting two antonymic ideas together to highlight contrasts; e.g., 'Give every man thine ear, but few thy voice.'
8. **Pathetic fallacy** – Technique where the environment reflects the emotions of the protagonist; e.g., 'The rain fell like teardrops.'
9. **Parenthesis** – Adding extra detail, through brackets, commas or dashes; e.g., 'happily forgo a society – that could not peaceably share a continent – for the rest of his natural life.'
10. **Assonance** – repetition of a vowel sound; e.g., 'I must confess, my quest, left me, depressed.'

In writing, paragraphs provide a structure and in your short story, you will frequently progress towards its' most exciting moment. You could begin by setting the scene and building tension which leads to the most dramatic part of the story. Then after the realisation of the most dramatic moment, you could provide a resolution whereby the story is concluded.

ASSESSMENT OBJECTIVES

The Assessment Objectives are not provided in the examination itself. However, I have provided which assessment objectives are being assessed in the practice questions in this book. It is important to be aware of the structure of how the assessment objectives are allocated in each question of the exam in order to maximise your opportunities to obtain full marks in each question.

It is often a good idea also to briefly plan your answer before you begin writing it. A plan will mean you answer the question in an organised and sequenced manner. Your newfound understanding of the assessment objectives will also ensure you have met all of the required criteria.

There are **two assessment objectives** assessed in the English Language Paper 1 Section B examination: **(AO5 = 24 marks for Content and Organisation; AO6 = 16 marks for Technical Accuracy)**.

<u>AO5 = Content and Organisation (24 marks)</u>

For a Grade 9:

Content: Communicate clearly, effectively and imaginatively. Select and adapt tone, style and register for different forms, purposes and audiences. Your communication must be convincing and compelling with an extensive and ambitious use of vocabulary and a sustained crafting of linguistic devices.

Organisation: Organise information and ideas, using structural and grammatical features to support coherence. Organisation will be provided through a varied and inventive use of structural features. Your writing must be compelling, incorporating a range of convincing and complex ideas and fluently link paragraphs with seamlessly integrated discourse.

AO6 = Technical Accuracy (16 marks)

For a Grade 9:

Technical Accuracy: Use a range of vocabulary and sentence structures for clarity, purpose and effect, combined with accurate spelling and punctuation. Sentence demarcation will be consistently secure and accurate with a wide range of punctuation, which is used with a high level of accuracy and provides impact to the writing. Use a full range of appropriate sentence forms for effect and use Standard English consistently and appropriately with a secure control of complex grammatical structures. Your essay must contain a high level of accuracy in spelling, including an extensive and ambitious use of vocabulary.

TIMINGS

In the AQA English Language GCSE Paper 1 and Paper 2 examinations there are 80 marks to aim for in 1 hour and 45 minutes (105 minutes). Please allocate the correct words per minute! Again, to re-iterate: The best approach is to spend 50 minutes on each question - 40 minutes writing and 10 minutes making notes, planning and checking your final answer for basic corrections at the end of the examination.

If you have extra time allocated to you, just change the calculation to accommodate the extra time you have i.e., if you have 25% extra time (= 50 minutes writing per question = 12 words per minute) and if you have 50% extra time (= 1 hour writing per question = 10 words per minute) this also equals a 600-word essay. Please **move on from the set question as soon as you have reached or are coming towards your time limit**. This ensures that you have excellent coverage of your whole exam and therefore attain a very good mark.

Similar to all the principles in this book, **you must apply and follow the correct timings for each question and stick to them throughout your exam to get an A star (Grade 9) in your English Language examinations.** Without applying this principle in these examinations (and to a large extent all examinations) you cannot achieve the highest marks! **Apply all of the principles provided in this book to succeed!**

APPROXIMATE WORD COUNT PER QUESTION

Now that you know what is on each examination, how the assessment objectives are assessed and the time allocated for each type of question; we come to what would be considered the correct word count per mark for each question. The primary principle though is to spend the right amount of time on each question.

In the answers in this book, I have provided the maximum word count theoretically possible for each answer which works out at **15 words per minute and per mark and this equals a 600-word essay**. If your answer has quality, this gives you the very best chance of obtaining the highest marks in your English Language exam. Obviously, it does not if you are waffling however. (Please remember to answer the question set and to move on in the time allocated.)

I am aware that some students can write faster than others but all students should be able to write 10 words per minute and thus a 400-word essay in the time (if they have not been allocated extra time). This is where conciseness is important in your writing.

My students and readers have applied all of the techniques of the Quality Control System™ I am providing you with; to gain A stars (Grade 9's) in their examinations. You can replicate them by following the advice in this book.

Thank you for purchasing this book and best wishes for your examinations! Joseph

AUTHOR'S NOTE

This book will provide you with 12 crystal clear and accurate examples of 'A' star grade (Grade 9) AQA GCSE English Language Paper 1 Section B: Creative Writing answers from the new syllabus and enables students to achieve the same grade in their upcoming examinations.

I teach both GCSE and A level English and Psychology and I am a qualified and experienced teacher and tutor of over 19 years standing. I teach, write and provide independent tuition in central and west London.

The resources in this book WILL help you to get an A star (Grade 9) in your GCSE English Language examinations, as they have done and will continue to do so, for my students.

Best wishes,

Joseph

ABOUT THE AUTHOR

I graduated from the Universities of Liverpool and Leeds and I obtained first class honours in my teacher training.

I have taught and provided private tuition for over 19 years up to university level. I also write academic resources for the Times Educational Supplement.

My tuition students, and now, my readers, have been fortunate enough to attain places to study at Oxford, Cambridge and Imperial College, London and other Russell Group Universities. The students have done very well in their examinations. I hope and know that my English Language, English Literature and Psychology books can enable you to take the next step on your academic journey.

Printed in Great Britain
by Amazon